Everything You _Never_ Want to Know About Camping

Everything You Never Want to Know About Camping

By BRUCE COCHRAN

WILLOW CREEK PRESS

Minocqua, Wisconsin

ISBN 1-57223-033-9

Published by   WILLOW CREEK PRESS
               P.O. Box 147
               Minocqua, WI 54548

For information on other Willow Creek titles,
write or call 1-800-850-WILD

Printed in the U.S.A.

For Holly and Wes

Never have your picture taken with a wild animal. He may be better looking than you.

Experienced campers know that birch bark is an effective backwoods deodorant. However, the bark will fall out when you raise your arms unless you secure it with duct tape.

Never wash your socks in the camp coffee. A good pair of socks is much too expensive to subject to such abuse.

No racks or ropes are needed for hauling the new peanut butter canoe. It sticks to the roof of your car.

When your teenage son wants to get his ears pierced, offer to do it for him with a grommet tool. Available from canvas suppliers and tent makers.

Take this simple test to see if you qualify for solo camping. Shine a flashlight into one ear. If the beam shines out the other ear you should not go into the woods alone.

If you suspect an item of food has been in the cooler too long, offer a small portion to your dog. If he eats it, so can you. If he rolls in it, pitch it.

The best backpacks are named for national parks or mountain ranges. Steer clear of those named for landfills or toxic waste sites.

There is nothing like a good camping trip to instill in children an appreciation for the wonders of nature.

New "truth in camping" legislation will prohibit manufacturers from including unwarranted claims in their advertising.

Parents should prepare for traveling with children by learning several simple games that can be played en route to their camping destination.

A good camping trip will get your kids outdoors and away from all that sex on television. Or will it?

When using a public campground, a tuba placed on your picnic table will help keep the campsites on either side vacant.

You can prevent longjohns that have lost their elasticity from slipping down by lining the crotch with Velcro.

Many wild animals in our national parks have been photographed so often it is no longer a novelty to them.

The sight of a bald eagle has thrilled campers for generations. The sight of a bald man, however, does absolutely nothing for the eagle.

Obese campers should always sleep on the center bed in a camper trailer, never on the outer beds which are supported only by aluminum rods.

That traditional campground treat, the wiener roast, will never be the same now that WONDER WEENIE is here. This King-sized version of the old favorite contains 50 pounds of beef lips and assorted unidentified animal parts. Feeds 25 adults or one teenager.

Hikers who carry their children on packframes should be discouraged from continuing the practice past the early years.

If the street lights in nearby towns go dim when you plug your motor home into an electrical hook-up you should switch to a smaller air conditioning unit and use your TV only during non-peak usage hours.

A beer can be kept cold by duct-taping it to your ex-wife's legs.

Always leave a campground with the same number of kids you entered with ... even if they're not the same ones.

In an emergency, it's okay to borrow small kitchen items from nearby campers. But don't overdo it.

It is possible to spend your entire vacation on a winding mountain road behind a large motor home.

Many public campgrounds allow you to call ahead and reserve a campsite.

Old socks can be made into high fiber jerky by smoking them over an open fire.

A camper who is proficient in the martial arts can cut a cord of firewood in an hour and is much quieter than a chainsaw.

A hot brick placed in your sleeping bag will keep your feet warm. A hot enchilada works almost as well but the cheese gets between your toes.

A message to litterbugs from Mother Nature —

To protect the environment, some public camp-grounds may soon enact ordinances that prohibit smoking OUTSIDE.

When rain forces you to stay in your tent for long periods, parents should set an example by maintaining a positive, cheerful attitude.

Responsible campers always teach their children that there is a right way and a wrong way to gather firewood.

Your dog will enjoy camping if he is properly housed. Large breeds will need a full-sized travel crate. Yorkies and chihuahuas can be stuffed in a bowling bag.

If you find yourself in a campground on Earth Day be sure to commemorate the occasion properly.

Many a camper has been left cold and dirty by relying on a solar heated shower bag during an eclipse.

You can survive in the wilderness by shooting small game with a slingshot made from the elastic waistband of your undershorts.

Good news for campers lost in a downpour — when you are rescued the prop wash from the helicopter will dry your clothes immediately.

Acupuncture was invented by a camper who found a porcupine in his sleeping bag.

When smoking a fish, never inhale.

A tasty bonus awaits you when your springtime camping trip turns into a mushroom hunting expedition.

While the Swiss Army Knife has been popular for years, the Swiss NAVY Knife has remained largely unheralded. Its single blade functions as a tiny canoe paddle.

Backpackers should always stay on established hiking trails and pay attention to the helpful signs posted along the way.

A mesh duffel bag with holes cut for your head and arms makes a dandy see-through blouse.

If you really want to get back to nature at its most primitive, camp NAKED. But don't try it in a public campground.

Experienced campers keep a sewing kit handy for emergency repairs to clothes and tents. The addition of a KNITTING kit will give you something to do on a rainy day.

Conscientious parents should realize that a child's first camping trip is an exciting time and show patience and understanding.

While a sharp axe can be used for shaving, you should never try it with a chainsaw.

Savvy old woodsmen have long known the secret of starting a fire without matches — a cigarette lighter and lots of charcoal starter fluid.

A new summer job program for teens pays sturdy young boys minimum wage to support hammocks in treeless campgrounds.

A magnum version of the popular fanny pack is available for campers with unusually large fannies.

Although portrayed as sinister in Halloween lore, bats are harmless creatures and there is no reason to fear them.

Effective 1/1/97 you will actually have to enlist in the Swiss Army to get a Swiss Army Knife.

Modern rainsuits made of fabrics that "breathe" enable campers to stay dry in a downpour. Rainsuits that sneeze, cough and belch, however, add absolutely nothing to the wilderness experience.

Lint from your navel makes a handy fire starter. (Be sure to remove it from your navel, first.)

The collapsible cot was invented by accident when a fat lady attempted to lie down on a NON-COLLAPSIBLE cot.

Some Southern campers steadfastly refuse to recognize the existence of the North Star.

A 4wd vehicle and a topo map will enable you to get lost and/or stuck in more remote areas than you ever thought possible.

If you cook French fries and Italian sausage in a Dutch oven you are to be commended for your commitment to diversity and multiculturalism.

You can start a fire without matches by eating Mexican food, then breathing on a pile of dry twigs.

Effective January 1, campers who insist on referring to insects as "bugs" must undergo 20 hours of sensitivity training.

Dry cow or buffalo chips make excellent fuel — for your campfire, not your lantern.

The traditional campground pastime of pitching horseshoes is now under attack by animal rights activists who want the shoes distributed to under-privileged horses.

Bears the have been fed too often may come to associate campgrounds with food and become a nuisance.

If you take your dog camping and he encounters a porcupine, try to discourage him from getting acquainted in the usual doggy manner.

On a very hot day you can actually brew coffee in your solar shower bag.

You'll never be lost if you remember that moss always grows on the north side of your compass.

Check the washing instructions before purchasing any item of apparel to be worn camping. Buy only those that read "Beat on rock in stream."

Bear bells provide an element of safety for campers and hikers in grizzly country. The tricky part is getting them on the bear.

While any good quality rainsuit will keep you reasonably dry, an effective lightning suit has yet to be developed.

Due to pressure from feminist groups, the Big Sur area of California, popular with campers and hikers, has been renamed the Big M'am area.

The winch on your sport utility vehicle can be used to pull an uncooperative cork from a champagne bottle.

It's common knowledge that you walk in a circle when you are lost, but few people realize that right handers walk clockwise, lefties counter-clockwise.

You can duplicate the warmth of a down-filled bed roll by climbing into a plastic garbage bag with several geese.

If you camp to escape air pollution, leave the family dog at home.

A travel crate for your pet boa constrictor can be made by sealing both ends of a 30-foot section of six-inch PVC pipe with sturdy wire mesh.

"Old growth" is a term used by environmentalists to refer to mature forests, not that stuff on your face when you've been camping for a week.

A camper suffering from hypothermia can be revived by showing him a photo of Heather Locklear.

Western trail riders who burned "cow chips" in their campfires soon learned to increase their fuel supply by giving their cattle a mild laxative at bedtime.

A large carp can be used for a pillow.

You can keep wild animals out of your food at night by eating it all yourself before you go to bed.

The "spots" on the spotted owl are actually pimples and usually clear up when the owl's sex life improves.

You can survive sub-zero temperatures by leaving your tent and seeking shelter in the motor home of a nearby camper.

You can compress the diameter of your rolled-up sleeping bag by running over it with your car.

A safety tip for cold weather campers — confused or lonely geese have been known to mate with down-filled sleeping bags.

Female campers are heralding the arrival of the polypropylene bikini. It doesn't cover much, but what it DOES cover it keeps REEEAAAL warm.

You'll never be awakened by the call of the loon if you have an unlisted telephone number.

Animal rights groups insist that chipmunks who beg in campgrounds be fed only nutritious morsels free of fat and cholesterol. No artery-clogging Ding-Dongs or Big Macs.

You can take a cue from experienced campers who suspend their food supply to keep it away from wild animals by suspending your liquor supply to keep it away from drunks.

When canoeing a river and looking for a gravel bar to eat lunch on, try to find one with a satellite dish and cold beer.

Never threaten to kick someone's butt while wearing tevas or birkenstocks.

Executive types who are ill at ease in the outdoors will feel more comfortable in the new black wingtip snowshoe.
(Also available for attorneys is the tassel loafer model.)

You can sometimes sneak your inflatable love doll past suspicious campground personnel by dressing her in a flannel shirt and putting a fishing rod in her hand.

Never belch toward your campfire while drinking cheap whiskey.

When camping, always wear a long-sleeved shirt. It gives you something to wipe your nose on.

The guitar of the noisy teenager at the next campsite makes excellent kindling when smashed over a boulder.

You can avoid campgrounds that cater to strange people by taking note of the graffiti on rocks and trees.

Couples who insist on setting up a tent together should make sure their hospitalization insurance is paid up and take along a marriage counselor.

You can save weight in your backpack by eliminating unnecessary items and taking only the essentials like whiskey and dirty magazines.

A sharp rap with a canoe paddle does wonders for the whiney kid who wants to go back to town and play video games.

Everything is relative. To a wino, a corkscrew is a survival tool.

The camper who captures a live specimen of "Bigfoot" will earn a fortune ... especially if he can teach him to carry a football.

You can get even with the bear who raided your grub box by kicking his favorite stump apart and eating all the ants out of it.

You can create a beachball by driving your sport utility vehicle into a tree or boulder firmly enough to inflate the air bag.

Mountain climbing is okay, up to a point.

If your motor home is equipped with a satellite dish you can offset your campground fees by charging your fellow campers an exorbitant fee to view sporting events.

You can make your campsite seem more homey by sticking inspirational sayings and children's drawings on your ice chest with little magnets.

If the TV in your motor home conks out, try going outdoors for a while. You might actually enjoy it.

The term, "Not a happy camper" was first used in reference to a man who found a bullhead in his fishnet underwear.

Trail bikers will welcome this handy new product — the bike helmet/dog bowl. Available in periwinkle, indigo marl, and carrara print.

The phrase, "Pitch a tent," has special meaning for disgusted campers — as in "Let's pitch this #@#!! tent and go to a motel."

A great deal of hostility can be released by using newspaper photos of politicians for camp toilet paper.

Contrary to popular opinion, "tree huggers" are environmental moderates, not extremists. The real extremists are the tree kissers and tree fondlers.

Your car will hold more camping gear if you leave your wife and kids at home and go alone.

While reluctantly accepting the scientific fact that only female mosquitoes bite, feminist leaders insist that they do so only to assuage years of oppression by their male counterparts.

Don't be disappointed when your two-man pup tent does not include two men or a pup.

Some campers are now reporting a militant new strain of "insect with an attitude" that appears to be unaffected by the traditional bug zapper.

For novice campers who miss the city, tapes are available featuring recorded sounds of traffic, sirens, construction and gunfire.

Next time you arrive at your favorite campsite to find it already taken by other campers, challenge them to a family fistfight.

America's first tent, the tepee, was brought to this country by its inventor, a traveling tent salesman named T. P. Jones. It was an instant hit with Native Americans who previously lived in hogans and were called Hogans Heroes.

A potato baked in the coals for one hour makes an excellent side dish. A potato baked in the coals for three hours makes an excellent hockey puck.

Native Americans (the first campers by the truest sense of the word) used dyes made from berries to color-code the poles of their tepees.

When camping above the tree line, take a fire plug along for your dog.

You think it's fun making a lantern with lightning bugs? How would you like it if someone stuffed YOU in a jar just because your butt glowed in the dark?

Never use bubble gum to patch a hole in an air mattress.

Although birds love unpopped popcorn you should never feed it to them on extremely hot days.

If you camp for solitude and tranquility, leave your cellular phone at home.

COCHRAN!

Never try to take a hike while wearing electric socks unless you have a very long extension cord.

When inconsiderate campers disturb your sleep by playing loud music late at night, take note: the sounds blasting from the offending boombox are NEVER classical.

If you really want to rough it, try camping with no bungee cords or duct tape.

A truckload of spoiled pizza, parked 50 yards downwind, will keep your campsite free of flies for several hours.

If the frustrating task of leveling your camper trailer becomes too stressful you can level the entire campground by calling in an airstrike.

When ants invade your campsite, make the best of the situation by developing an ant farm. You'll derive hours of enjoyment from watching these industrious creatures drive their tiny tractors and combines.

Fair-skinned campers can screen out radiation with ECLIPSE IN A TUBE, the new Chernobyl-strength sunblock.

Tired of roughing it in the conventional motor home? Move up to MOTOR MANSION. Complete with five bedrooms, three fireplaces, and a 30-year mortgage.

The new STEP ONE water purifier forces water through a screen to filter out the largest particles of pollution. "At least I didn't choke on the big hunks" claims one satisfied user from his hospital bed.

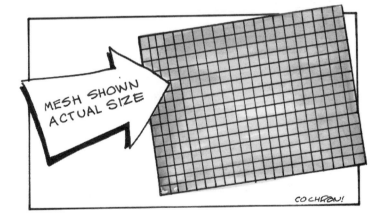

If your teenager thinks snowshoes are dorky-looking, introduce him to the new SNOW SNEAKER. Available in sizes 30 to 55 EEEEE.

In an emergency, the drawstring from a hood or jacket can be used to strangle a snoring tentmate.

Don't let insects mar your camping fun. Use BLAST-A-BUG. Guaranteed to repel flies, mosquitoes and ticks.
EXTRA STRENGTH BLAST-A-BUG also repels birds, bats and low-flying aircraft.

Cost-conscious campers will welcome the new BUTTBULB. It harnesses that most obnoxious (and heretofore useless) of all substances to provide economical lighting while eliminating offensive odors. Intensity may vary with your dog's diet and intestinal condition.

Never take your cat to a beachfront campground.

Campers who "couldn't hurt a fly" will love the new BUG SENTENCER. Rather than merely "zapping" insects, it incarcerates them until they have paid their debt to society.

Campers who can't stay off the information highway will welcome the new generation of computers and FAX machines that operate on propane.

A new insecticide claims to kill ticks and mosquitoes for two weeks. It is not clear what miraculous force brings them back to life at the end of this period.

The National Camping Health Organization has just released this official camp food pyramid showing its recommendations for the healthy camper's diet.

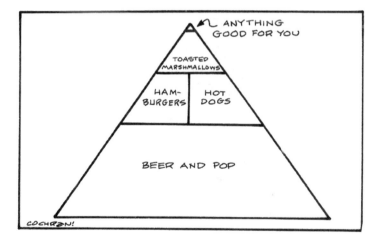

Teenage campers will welcome the new all-ter-rain skateboard. It features outsize tires with raised white letters and a $5,000 accidental injury policy.

The CANOE paddle, a simple device used to propel a boat, should not be confused with the GNU paddle, a similar device used by Tibetan veterinarians as a tongue depressor.

For the cost-conscious camper who doesn't require a lot of space, the bed of a pick-up truck makes dandy sleeping quarters: CAUTION: never try it while driving.

Though it is not generally known, park rangers can perform weddings. If you choose to be married in a public campground you must use lantern mantels for rings and promise to raise your children as tree huggers.

Cost-conscious campers can take a tip from race car drivers and partially defray expenses by soliciting corporate sponsors for their trips.

Yellowstone personnel claim that some city-bred visitors think old faithful is man-made and inquire about the plumbing. These same people probably also think Mt. Rushmore is a natural rock formation.

Fry bats, wilt mature trees and realign planets with the amazing new SUN GUN, a 10-billion candlepower hand-held spotlight. Plug it into a powerline or any nearby nuclear plant.

Several cigar butts added to the hickory or mesquite in your smoker will add an aroma and flavor that your family won't soon forget.

Many public campgrounds have identification signs posted in strategic locations to help you increase your knowledge of the outdoors.

No more messy misfires on those midnight latrine trips with ILLUMI-LOAD, the personal belt-on spotlight that illuminates the target area.

A well-known sculptor will soon begin carving the likeness of Madonna into a Western mountainside. It will be known as Mt. Raunchmore.

Liven up those camp meals with cornbread sticks shaped like Madonna, Elvis and Nixon with this new cast iron baking pan.

No conscientious outdoorsman would ever wash his truck in a stream, many of which now contain enough toxic waste to eat paint, brake lines and possibly pit windshields.

No need to invest in an expensive high-tech camp grill when an old refrigerator shelf will do. Just drink four quick beers when you arrive at your campsite (one to support each corner of the shelf) and you're ready to cook.

In addition to being a trusty timepiece, the new WRAMBO WRIST COMPUTER features a calendar, alarm, altimeter, moon and tide display, solunar table, compass, barometer, thermometer, global positioning system and registers earthquakes up to 7.5 Richter. Weight, 12 pounds.